Home is Where the Marine Corps Sends You

Camp Lejeune, North Carolina

By Melissa Davis

Illustrated by Juli Dorton

HAPPY OWL PUBLISHING™

Published by Happy Owl Publishing TM

ISBN 978-1497592407

Edited by Rebekah Sanderlin

Designed and produced by Scott Stevens

Special thanks to Claire Woodward, military family advocate, for ideas about which locations should be featured in this book.

For more information, and to purchase additional copies, visit our website
www. HomeIsWhereBooks.com

Contact the author by email: Melissa@HomeIsWhereBooks.com

For my Grandma, my rock

Melissa Davis

Mandy sat at her desk, quietly struggling to focus on Mrs. Bishop, her 5th grade teacher. The lesson was about fractions, something Mandy needed to understand, but she just could not concentrate. The clock on the side wall said it was 10:30 in the morning.

"Only six more hours," thought Mandy. "Everything will be different in just six more hours."

"What do we call the top number in a fraction, Mandy?" asked Mrs. Bishop... "Mandy," she repeated. "Mandy!"

"Ummm, the numerator," Mandy answered, when she finally heard her teacher.

"Nice job. You seemed a million miles away. Are you alright?" questioned Mrs. Bishop.

"Yes," Mandy replied. "I was just thinking about something else. Today is a special day."

"OK, well please pay attention," Mrs. Bishop said as she moved on to the next question.

The rest of the school day crept by slowly for Mandy. Not being able to concentrate, watching the clock, and fighting back her nervous excitement made the day seem to last a hundred years. But finally, at 2:30 p.m., the school bell rang and it was time to go home.

Mandy was in a hurry, so she packed up quickly and was the first student to board bus 183.

6

"Only two more hours now," contemplated Mandy as she sat on the bus waiting for the rest of the kids to board.

The ride home, just like the school day, seemed to last forever. The bus got stuck behind every slow driver and had to stop at every long red light.

" I am NEVER going to get there," Mandy wanted to scream. "Why should kids have to go to school on such a special day?" she pouted.

This day was special, not just for Mandy, but for her whole family, and all she wanted to do was be with them right now.

The bus stopped to let off two little boys.

"Four more stops," thought Mandy. "Now three, now two, only one more..."

She dashed to the front of the bus! It was her stop!

"Aren't you forgetting something?" asked Mr. Henry, the bus driver.

"My book bag!"

183

8

Mandy walked as quickly
as she could back to her
seat to get the bag;
her excitement was
almost unbearable.

"Good day!" chirped
Mr. Henry.

"Bye!" yelled Mandy from
halfway down her
driveway.   9

When Mrs. Oakwood opened the door to greet her daughter, she almost got trampled. "Mom," panted Mandy, "Is Daddy here yet? Did he call you? Can we just go to his work?"

"Whoa, girl!" laughed Mrs. Oakwood. "Your father isn't here yet. He should be home soon, and he will have a clue with him about where we will be going next. It's tradition. Now let's get you unpacked..."

Today was the day that Sgt. Oakwood received his orders about where they would be stationed next. Every three or four years, their family moved to a new Marine base. It was scary to leave friends and neighbors and start over, but Mandy had come to love the adventures that came with being the daughter of a Marine.

Eric, Mandy's little brother, sat on the kitchen floor building forts out of blocks. "I can't wait for Dad to come home," he said.

"He'll be here soon," Mrs. Oakwood reassured her son.   11

"This is officially the longest day in history," Mandy told her mother.

"Where do you think we'll go?" asked Mrs. Oakwood.
"Any guesses?"

"Oh, I think it will be somewhere amazing," said Mandy. "Maybe we can even move to another country!"

About that time, Mandy heard a truck door slam.

"He's here!" she yelled as she darted to the front door. Eric chased behind her.

Sgt. Oakwood was smiling to himself as he gathered his things out of his little red truck.

"Daddy! Hurry up! I didn't think you would ever get here!" shouted Mandy.

"Come on, Daddy!" Eric begged.

"I'm coming, I'm coming," said Sgt. Oakwood. "You two get Mom and wait for me in in the family room."

13

Mandy could hardly breathe. She felt happy and sad and excited and scared all at the same time. As she sat down on the couch beside her mother, Mandy suddenly realized that maybe she didn't want to move. What about her friends? Her teachers? Her great school?

Too late. Sgt. Oakwood walked into the family room with something behind his back. This was the tradition. When he got his orders, he would bring home a "clue" to help his family guess their new duty station.

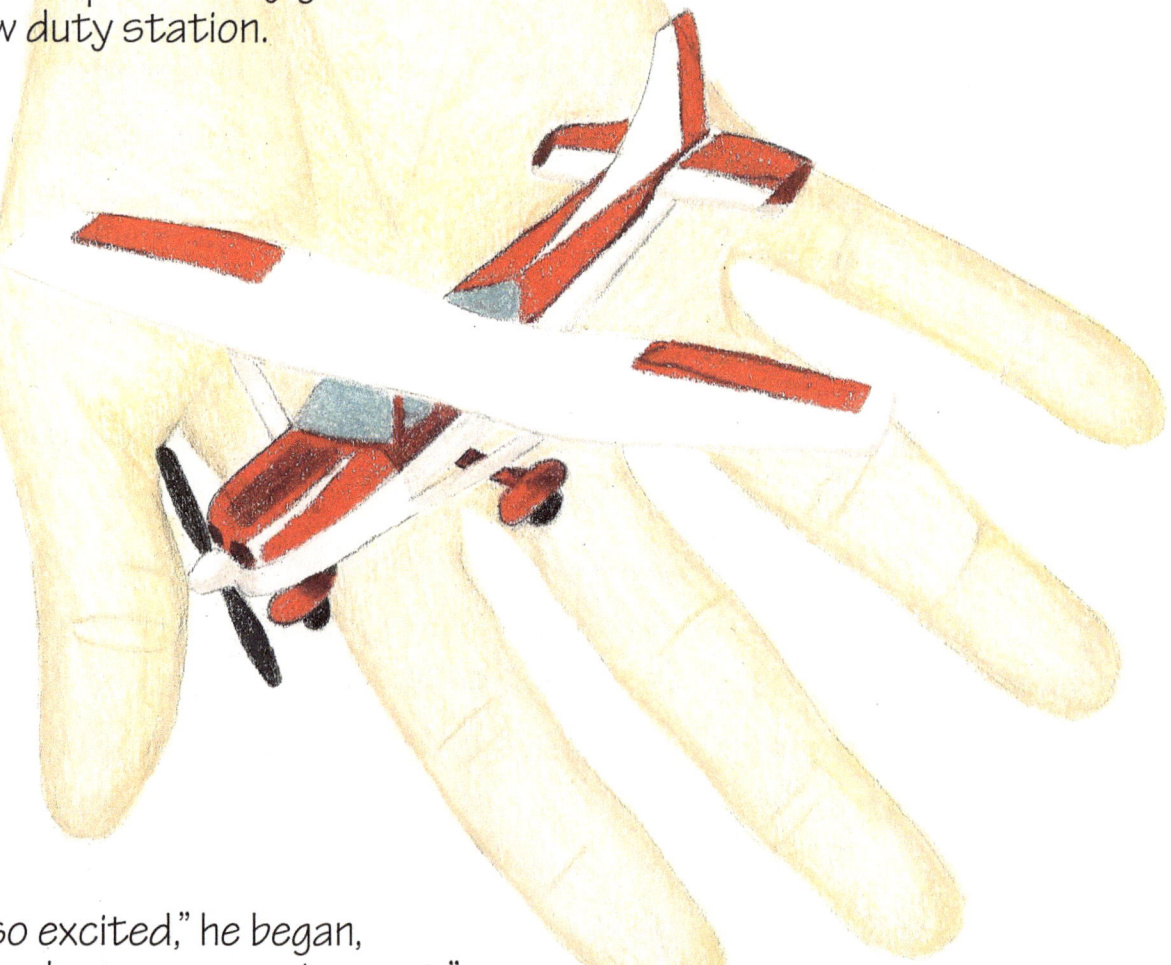

"I am so excited," he began, "about where we are going next." Mandy's father pulled his hand out from its hiding place and opened it to reveal a little toy airplane.

Mandy was confused. "Are we moving to an airport?" she asked.

"No, silly," Explained her dad. "We are moving to the home of the first airplane flight!"

"Oh...," Mrs. Oakwood smiled. She had figured it out.

"I know the Wright Brothers were the first people to fly," said Mandy, "but I don't know where they were."

"I don't know, either!" exclaimed Eric. "Just tell us!"

15

"I still don't know," Mandy said, frustrated.

"All right, all right.
Do you know, Dear?"
he turned to his wife.

Mrs. Oakwood
guessed, "Is it
Camp Lejeune,
North Carolina?"

"Bingo!!!" he shouted.

"The Wright Brothers flew their first airplane at Kitty Hawk, North Carolina," Mandy's father explained. "Kitty Hawk is located on a beautiful chain of beaches called the Outer Banks. We will only live a few hours from there. We can go and see where the first airplane flight occurred."

"That's right," said Mrs. Oakwood.
"North Carolina license plates even say
'First in Flight' on them!"

"You kids are going to love Camp Lejeune!" exclaimed Sgt. Oakwood.
"Go get me the map."

Mandy ran to the den and opened the second drawer of the filing cabinet. There she found the United States map that her family always used when they got orders to go to a new place.

She bounced back into the family room with the old treasure and presented it to her father.

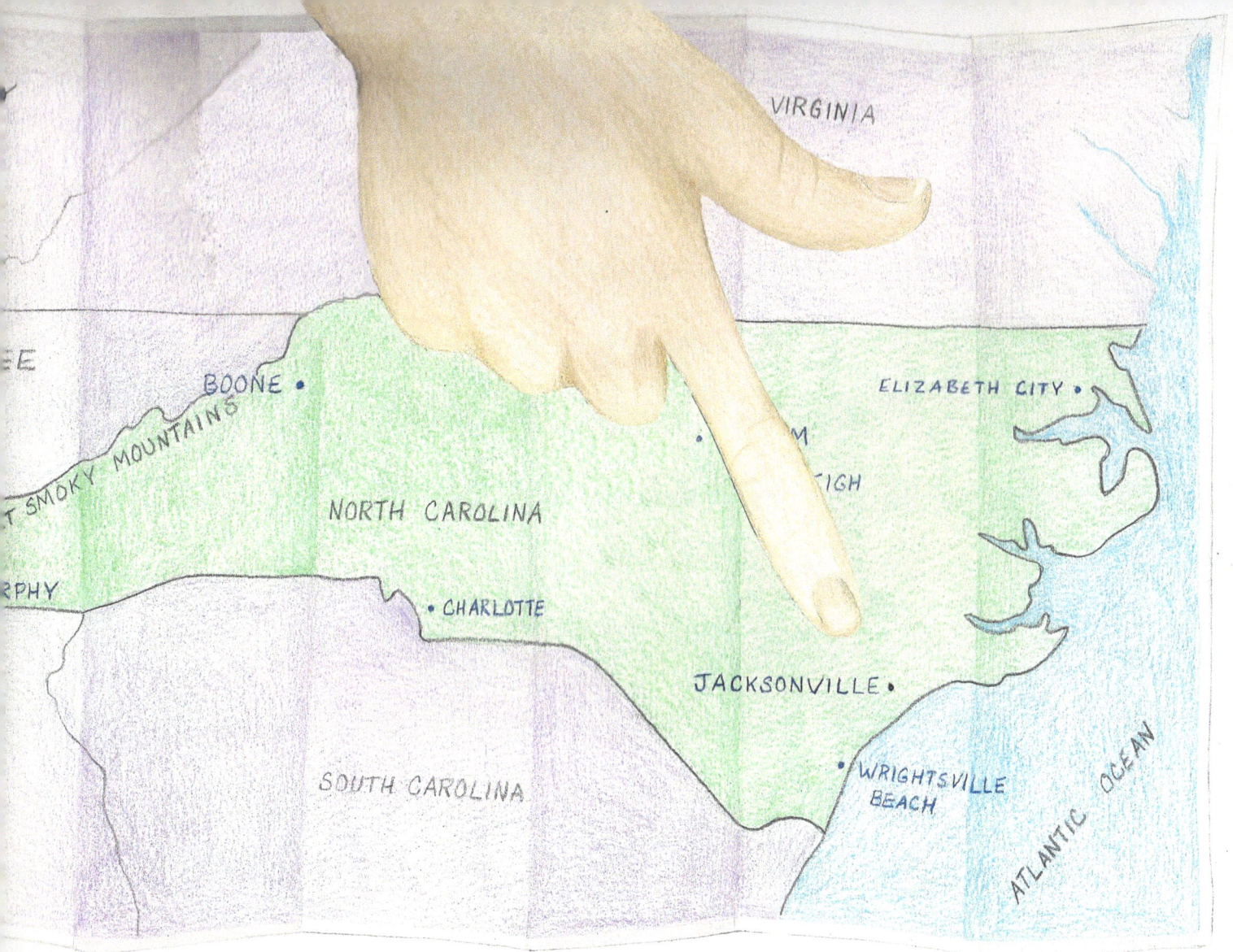

Sgt. Oakwood carefully opened the map and pointed to city that was on the east coast of North Carolina.

"Camp Lejeune is located in Jacksonville, North Carolina," he explained. "Jacksonville is named after Andrew Jackson. He was the 7th president of the United States."

19

"As you can see, we will be stationed very close to the ocean. Onslow Beach is located right on Camp Lejeune, and we can go there to get suntans and to find shark teeth!"

"Cool! The beach!" exclaimed Eric. He could not wait to build huge sand castles and ride the waves.

"How exciting!" added Mandy. The beach was one of her favorite places in the whole world.

" Camp Lejeune is only about an hour from the great city of Wilmington, North Carolina," said Sgt. Oakwood.

"Are there fun things to do in Wilmington?" asked Mandy.

"Yes! I can't wait to show you guys the USS North Carolina. It's a huge battleship that we can go in and explore!"

Eric ran to his room and grabbed his toy battleship. When he returned he asked, "Will the USS North Carolina look like this?"

Mrs. Oakwood laughed, "That's right son, but it will be much, much bigger!"

"Wilmington is also home to Screen Gem Studios," their father told them. "Movies and TV Shows are made there!"

"No way!" exclaimed Mandy. She immediately thought of becoming an actress. "Can we be in a movie?" she wondered aloud.

"Maybe you can do that one day," answered Sgt. Oakwood, "but when we visit you will have to settle for taking a tour."

"We might meet some famous people, though," Eric said, trying to reassure his big sister.

Sgt. Oakwood laughed at his son. Then he continued, "Pine Knoll Shores is also a great place to visit when we get to Camp Lejeune."

"I heard that there is a huge aquarium there," said Mrs. Oakwood.
"I love aquariums!" announced Mandy.
"Me too! Maybe we will see some sharks!" Eric added.

23

"Another place that we must visit is Tryon Palace," said Sgt. Oakwood. "It is located in the beautiful city of New Bern, North Carolina."

"Tell us about it, Daddy!" begged Mandy.

The soldier smiled. His kids were getting excited about the move to Camp Lejeune. "Tryon Palace was the first governor's mansion in North Carolina. We can take a tour of the mansion and the gardens; then we can buy some souvenirs at the museum."

"What's a mansion?" questioned Eric.

"It's a really, really big house! Like as big as ten or fifteen regular houses," explained Mrs. Oakwood.

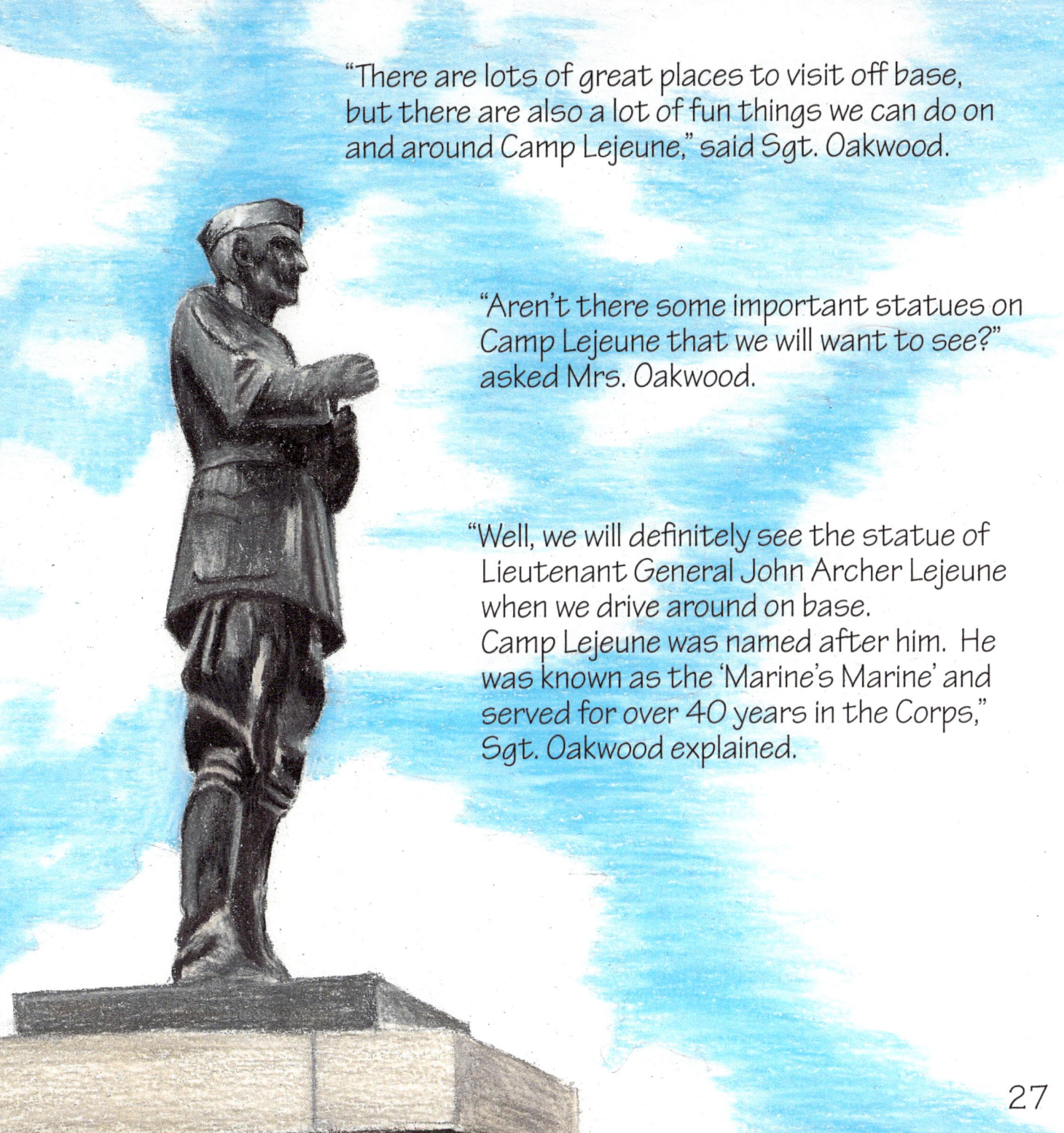

"There are lots of great places to visit off base, but there are also a lot of fun things we can do on and around Camp Lejeune," said Sgt. Oakwood.

"Aren't there some important statues on Camp Lejeune that we will want to see?" asked Mrs. Oakwood.

"Well, we will definitely see the statue of Lieutenant General John Archer Lejeune when we drive around on base. Camp Lejeune was named after him. He was known as the 'Marine's Marine' and served for over 40 years in the Corps," Sgt. Oakwood explained.

"Also," he continued, "it will be important to visit the Beirut Memorial. It was built on Camp Lejeune in 1986 to honor 271 Marines who lost their lives trying to spread freedom and help the people of Beirut, Lebanon."

"How sad for those Marines and their families," said Mandy.

"It was a sad time, but those Marines were heroes, so it is great that there is a monument to remember them," explained Sgt. Oakwood.

"There is also a Vietnam Memorial on Camp Lejeune," added Mrs. Oakwood. "It was built to remember all the Marines that lost their lives fighting for our country in Vietnam."

"Both of these monuments are important for you guys to see and learn about," stated Sgt. Oakwood. "They are a part of the great history of the Marine Corps."

It was obvious that Sgt. Oakwood had done some research about his new duty station. He liked to be prepared so he could help his children get excited about moving to new places with him. The father of two knew that moving frequently was a hardship on his kids, but he also knew that they were growing stronger and wiser with each relocation. He was determined to make military life a grand family adventure. His children were getting the opportunity to see the world, one Marine base at a time, and that made him proud to be a Marine.

"Let's have dinner," Mrs. Oakwood announced, marking a pause in their family discussion. "We can talk more about Camp Lejeune over spaghetti and salads!"

Dinner was wonderful, and Mandy and Eric talked non-stop about the upcoming move. They had tons of questions for their father.

Mandy found out that there would be a movie theater with a balcony on Camp Lejeune where she could have birthday parties.

She was also delighted when her father told her that there were places in Jacksonville and on the base where she could take horseback riding lessons.

30

Eric discovered that there would be lots of opportunities for fishing at New River on Camp Lejeune.

He also found out that they would live near a race track where he could go to watch drag car races.

After dinner, Mrs. Oakwood gave Mandy the address to Jacksonville's Chamber of Commerce so she could write them and request brochures. Sgt. Oakwood sat at the computer with Eric and showed him pictures of Wilmington and Camp Lejeune on the Internet.

" This has been a great night," said Sgt. Oakwood. "I do have something else in my brief case, though, that I must get out before we all go to bed."

"What is it, Daddy?" Eric wanted to know.

"Oh, is it another clue about Camp Lejeune?" Mandy asked.

"No, actually this is a little something for your mother," he replied.

"Me?" Mrs. Oakwood looked pleasantly surprised.

Sgt. Oakwood pulled a small wooden heart out of his brief case and handed it to his wife. She carefully turned it over and began grinning from ear to ear. The heart said "Camp Lejeune, North Carolina" on it.

"Oh thank you, dear," she said to him as she walked across the family room to the plaque hanging on the wall.

Mrs. Oakwood gently connected the heart to the bottom of a long chain of hearts that hung down from a wooden house that said, "Home is Where the Marine Corps Sends You." This would be the fourth Marine base she would take her family to, so it was now the fourth heart on the chain. Each one had the name of a Marine base on it where her family had lived.

34

"Do you remember what your father and I always tell you before we move?" Mrs. Oakwood asked her children as she sat back down on the couch with them.

"I do," said Mandy. "No matter where we go, one thing never changes - our family. We will always have each other when everything else is strange and scary and new."

"That is exactly right," said Sgt. Oakwood. "Now you two need to get to bed. We have had quite enough excitement for one night." He kissed Mandy and Eric on their foreheads and gave them each a quick hug.

"This is going to be fun," he called to them as they headed down the hallway.

35

Mandy crawled into her bed thinking about all the things her father had told her about Camp Lejeune. "Daddy is right; this is going to be fun," she thought as she dozed off into a peaceful sleep.

Mrs. Oakwood sat on the edge of Eric's bed.

"Are you excited, honey?" she asked him as she straightened his covers.

"Oh yes, Mom," Eric yawned. "I can't wait to tell everyone at school tomorrow that I am going to see Blackbeard's treasure in North Carolina." He grinned up at his mother, and then he closed his eyes.

37

As she closed her son's door, Mrs. Oakwood smiled. She really did look forward to moving to Camp Lejeune, North Carolina and having yet another family adventure.

After you read, think about...

What are some things you can do to help new students feel welcome when they move to your school?

Mandy's father said his children were getting stronger and wiser with each relocation. What do you think he meant?

How many other states have access to both the beach and the mountains?

When kids have to move, what are some ways they can stay in touch with their friends?

Facts About North Carolina

The capital of North Carolina is Raleigh.

North Carolina became the 12th state to join the union in 1789.

The largest city in North Carolina is Charlotte.

North Carolina is the largest producer of sweet potatoes in the nation.

The state flower of North Carolina is the dogwood.

Krispy Kreme Doughnuts was founded in Winston-Salem, North Carolina.

Pepsi was invented and first served in New Bern, North Carolina in 1898.

James K. Polk, born in Mecklenburg County, North Carolina, was the 11th president of the United States.

The North Carolina General Assembley of 1987 adopted milk as the official state beverage.

North Carolina's state bird is the cardinal.

The oldest town in North Carolina is Bath, which was incorporated in 1705.

North Carolina has 1,500 lakes of 10 acres or more in size and 37,000 miles of fresh water streams.

A nationally-famous cuisine from North Carolina is pork barbecue.

North Carolina's state motto is "Esse quam videri," which means "To be, rather than to seem."

www.ingramcontent.com/pod-product-compliance
Lightning Source LLC
Chambersburg PA
CBHW060837290526
45792CB00006BB/1967